D1303622

This library edition published in 2011 by Walter Foster Publishing, Inc.
Walter Foster Library
Distributed by Black Rabbit Books.
P.O. Box 3263 Mankato, Minnesota 56002

Printed in China by CT PRINTING, Shenzhen.

First Library Edition

Library of Congress Cataloging-in-Publication Data

Learn to draw Walt Disney's Mickey Mouse. -- 1st library ed.
    p. cm.
  ISBN 978-1-936309-02-3 (hardcover)
 1. Cartoon characters--Juvenile literature. 2. Mickey Mouse (Fictitious
character)--Juvenile literature. 3. Drawing--Technique--Juvenile
literature. I. Walter Foster (Firm) II. Title: Walt Disney's Mickey Mouse.
III. Title: Disney's Mickey Mouse.
  NC1764.L37 2011
  741.5'1--dc22
                                                                2010005330

Illustrated and designed by John Loter and the Disney Publishing Creative Development
Staff

022010
0P1816

9 8 7 6 5 4 3 2 1

LEARN TO DRAW

WALT DISNEP'S

MICKEY MOUSE

WELCOME

Hi! It's your old pal Mickey!

Do ya like to draw? I sure do! It's a lot of fun! This book will help you become an even better artist than you are now!

I've opened my sketchbook with all the secret information—how tall Goofy is . . . how to draw Minnie's shoes. . . . It's easy when you know how! The whole gang is gonna help you out along the way. I'll meet you at the end of the book!

MICKEY

THE GANG

Before we get started, let's get to know Mickey and his friends.

MICKEY MOUSE

Mickey Mouse is always friendly and outgoing. Everybody likes him.

MINNIE MOUSE

Minnie Mouse is Mickey Mouse's sweetheart and friend.

DONALD DUCK

Donald Duck has quite a temper, but he's still lots of fun to be around.

Check out how big (or small) the characters are compared to one another. When you draw them together, you'll want to make sure that you don't make Donald taller than Goofy! Remember that everyone is just about the same height except Goofy, who's the tallest.

DAISY DUCK

GOOFY

PLUTO

Daisy Duck is Donald's favorite gal. She's quite fashionable.

Goofy is a pretty silly guy. Make sure you draw him having lots of fun.

Pluto's one happy pup! His best pal is Mickey Mouse, who also happens to be his owner.

Before learning to draw the characters, it's a good idea to get warmed up. Start by drawing simple shapes like circles and ovals. Don't worry about making them perfect; just keep your wrist nice and loose. When you feel comfortable with your shapes, move on to the steps.

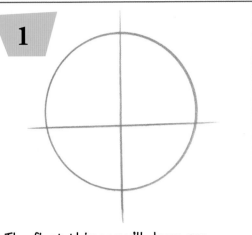

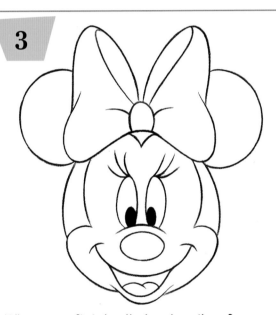

Usually artists draw characters in several steps. Sometimes the steps are different, depending on what you're drawing. The important thing to remember is to start simply and add details later. The blue lines show each new step, and the black lines show what you've already drawn.

1

The first thing you'll draw are guidelines to help postion the features of the character.

2

Next you'll start to add details to your drawing. It will take several steps to add all the details.

3

When you finish all the details of your drawing, you can go back and erase your guidelines. You can also darken your lines with a pen or marker.

Goofy's learned all the steps, and now he's ready to paint the finished drawing!

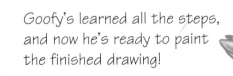

MICKEY MOUSE
Drawing Mickey's Face

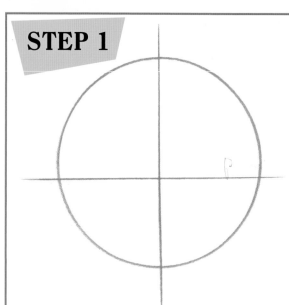

Start with a circle. Add center lines to help position Mickey's features.

STEP 2

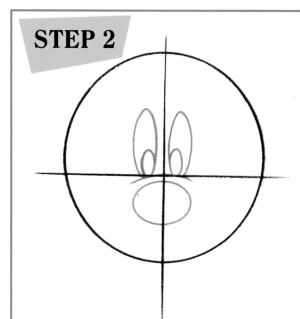

Now add Mickey's eyes and nose. His eyes rest on the edge of one center line. Add a little curve right below his eyes.

STEP 3

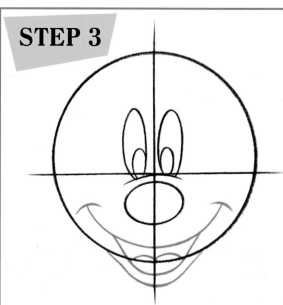

Add Mickey's smile and chin. The top portion of his mouth follows the same curve as his nose. See how his chin extends below the circle of his head.

Pluto is Mickey's favorite pup, and Mickey is Pluto's best pal.

STEP 4

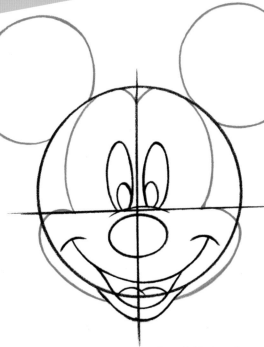

Draw two large ovals for Mickey's ears. Add curved lines to form the area around his cheeks and eyes. (This is called the "mask.")

STEP 5

Erase your guidelines and clean up the drawing.

STEP 6

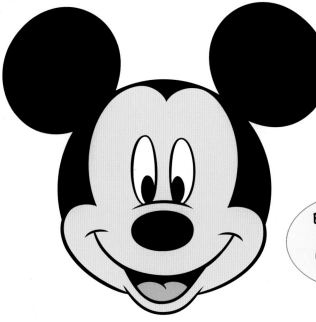

Now color your drawing of Mickey.

BE SURE TO MAKE HIM HANDSOME!

MICKEY MOUSE
Drawing Mickey's Body

When drawing the characters' bodies, notice the curved line going from top to bottom in Step 1. This line is called the **line of action**. The line of action is a guideline to give your character direction and movement.

STEP 1

Start with a circle. Add a pear shape for Mickey's body. Mickey's height is 2-1/2 times the size of his head.

STEP 2

Add Mickey's arms, legs, hands, and feet.

When the tops of Mickey's hands show, be sure to add the stitching lines to his gloves!

STEP 3

Add Mickey's ears, pants, and shoes.

STEP 4

Fill in all the details for Mickey's face that you learned on pages 8 and 9. Don't forget to add his tail!

STEP 5

Erase your guidelines and clean up the drawing.

STEP 6

Now color your drawing of Mickey.

Mickey's shoes are slightly longer than his hands.

MINNIE MOUSE
Drawing Minnie's Face

Start with a circle. Add center lines to help position Minnie's features, just as you did for Mickey.

STEP 2

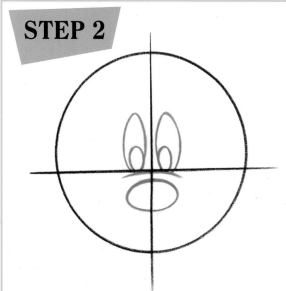

Add Minnie's eyes and nose. Her eyes rest on the edge of one center line.

STEP 3

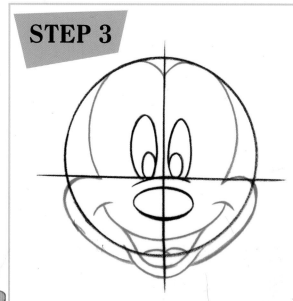

Add Minnie's smile and chin. The top portion of her mouth follows the same curve as her nose. See how her chin extends below the circle of her head. Add curved lines to form the mask.

Minnie and Daisy are the very best of friends.

STEP 4

Draw two large ovals for Minnie's ears and a great big bow on top of her head. Don't forget her eyelashes!

Don't forget Minnie's eyelashes. The middle lashes are longer than the others.

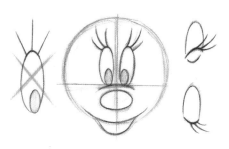

STEP 5

Erase your guidelines and clean up the drawing.

STEP 6

Now color your drawing of Minnie.

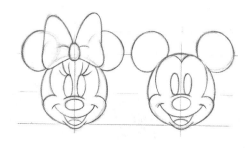

Minnie's and Mickey's heads are similar, but Minnie's eyes are slightly larger and wider than Mickey's. Her open mouth is slightly smaller than his.

13

MINNIE MOUSE
Drawing Minnie's Body

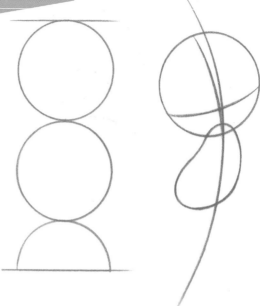

Start with a circle. Add a bean shape for Minnie's body. Minnie's height is 2-1/2 times the size of her head.

STEP 2

Add Minnie's arms, legs, hands, and feet.

Minnie's shoes have a wide, pointed toe and thick, high heels.

STEP 3

Add Minnie's ears, dress, bow, and shoes.

14

STEP 4

Fill in all the details for Minnie's face that you learned on pages 12 and 13. Don't forget to add her tail!

STEP 5

Erase your guidelines and clean up the drawing.

STEP 6

Now color your drawing of Minnie.

15

DONALD DUCK

Drawing Donald's Face

STEP 1

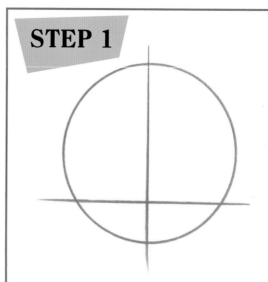

Start with a circle. Add center lines to help position the features.

STEP 2

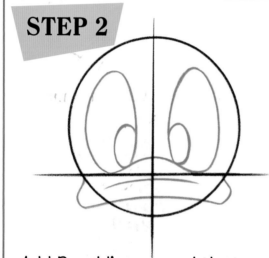

Add Donald's eyes and the top of his bill. His eyes rest on the edge of one center line. Draw the curved lines for his bill.

STEP 3

Add Donald's eyebrows and tufts on the top of his head. See how his lower bill curves below his head. His cheeks are very curvy when he smiles. Now add a little triangle for his tongue.

Goofy's silly attitude sometimes irritates the hot-tempered Donald, but Mickey usually manages to keep the peace.

16

STEP 4

Add Donald's cap. See how the hatband and the ribbon are the same width.

STEP 5

Erase your guidelines and clean up the drawing.

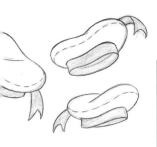

Donald's hat is soft and flexible but always holds its shape.

STEP 6

Now color your drawing of Donald.

GAWRSH! THAT'S A FUNNY HAT!

DONALD DUCK
Drawing Donald's Body

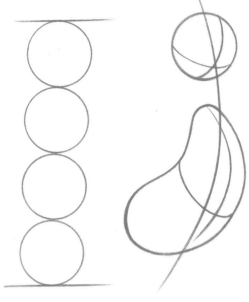

STEP 1

Start with a circle. Add a jelly bean shape for Donald's body. Donald's height is about 4 times the size of his head.

STEP 2

Add Donald's arms, legs, hands, feet, and bill.

Donald's hands are almost as long as the height of his head.

STEP 3

Sketch in Donald's clothes.

18

STEP 4

Draw Donald's features as you learned on pages 16 and 17. Add the details of his clothes. Don't forget his tail!

STEP 5

Erase your guidelines and clean up the drawing.

STEP 6

Now color your drawing of Donald.

19

DAISY DUCK
Drawing Daisy's Face

STEP 1

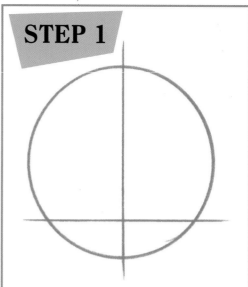

Start with a circle. Add cross lines to help position Daisy's features.

STEP 2

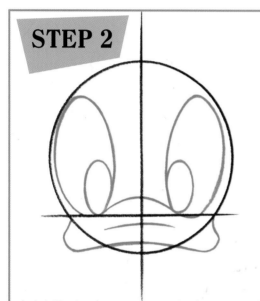

Add Daisy's eyes and the top of her bill. Notice how her eyes are rounder and more angled than Donald's. The bottoms of her eyes and the top of her bill fit together smoothly.

STEP 3

Add Daisy's eyebrows and the lower part of her bill. Now add the little triangle for her tongue, just as you did for Donald.

Daisy is just crazy for Donald.

STEP 4

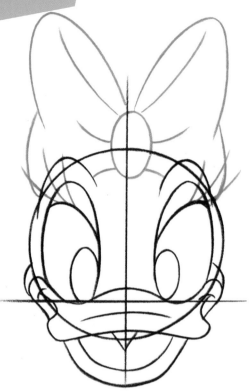

Add Daisy's bow and eyelashes. She has three eyelashes over each eye. The middle lashes are longer than the others.

STEP 5

Erase your guidelines and clean up the drawing.

STEP 6

Now color your drawing of Daisy.

BETTER SHARPEN YOUR PENCIL FOR DAISY'S EYELASHES!

DAISY DUCK
Drawing Daisy's Body

STEP 1

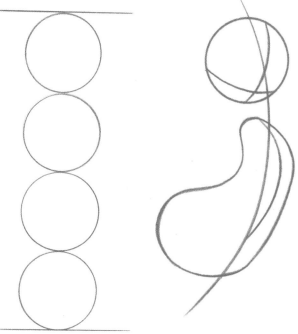

Start with a circle. Add a curved pear shape for Daisy's body. Daisy's height is about 4 times the size of her head.

STEP 2

Add Daisy's arms, legs, hands, feet, and bill.

Daisy's bracelet hangs loosely from her left wrist.

STEP 3

Sketch in Daisy's clothes. Don't forget her bracelet.

STEP 4

Fill in all the details of Daisy's head and clothes. Add a small tuft of feathers for her tail.

STEP 5

Erase your guidelines and clean up the drawing.

STEP 6

Now color your drawing of Daisy.

If you curve or tilt Daisy's body and head, she can look flirtatious, happy, or surprised.

GOOFY
Drawing Goofy's Face

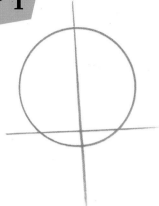

Start with a circle. Then add cross lines as shown to help position Goofy's features. In this expression, part of Goofy's face is on an angle, so you'll make the center lines angled, too.

STEP 2

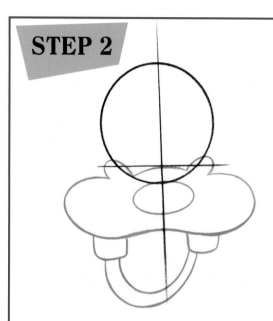

Add a squished oval beneath the circle for Goofy's nose. Then add his cheeks, teeth, and mouth.

STEP 3

Add Goofy's big oval eyes and tongue.

Goofy's head is similar to Pluto's.

24

STEP 4

Add Goofy's hat and ears. His ears are like big teardrops.

STEP 5

Erase your guidelines and clean up the drawing.

STEP 6

Now color your drawing of Goofy.

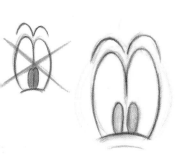

Notice how the whites of Goofy's eyes touch each other. Just make sure you keep his pupils separate.

Goofy's hat is about 1 head long. It's squishy looking and leans to one side.

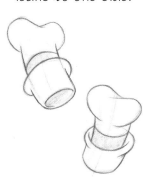

25

GOOFY
Drawing Goofy's Body

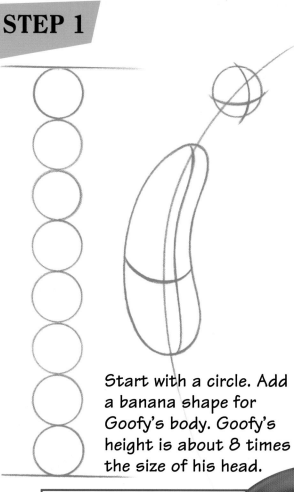

Start with a circle. Add a banana shape for Goofy's body. Goofy's height is about 8 times the size of his head.

STEP 2

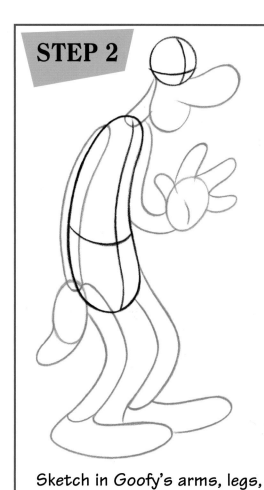

Sketch in Goofy's arms, legs, hands, feet, and head.

Goofy has BIG feet.

The toes of his shoes turn up slightly.

STEP 3

Add Goofy's clothes.

STEP 4

Fill in the details of Goofy's face and clothes.

se Goofy's entire ody to act out a mood or action.

STEP 5

Erase your guidelines and clean up the drawing.

Goofy's loose-limbed body is capable of a wide variety of poses.

STEP 6

Now color your drawing of Goofy.

PLUTO
Drawing Pluto's Body

STEP 1

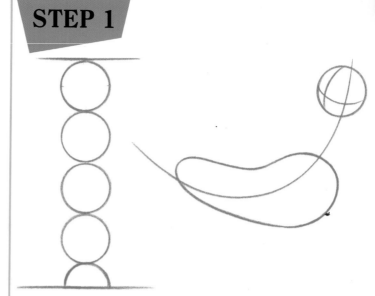

Start with a circle. Add a pear shape for Pluto's body. Pluto's height is about 4-1/2 times the size of his head.

STEP 2

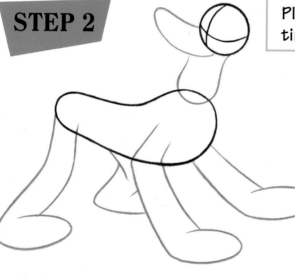

Sketch in Pluto's legs and head.

STEP 3

Start to add Pluto's face and ears. Sketch in his collar and add some detail to his feet for his toes.

Pluto has three pads on the bottom of each paw.

His three toes are stubby.

STEP 4

Fill in all the details for Pluto's head. Don't forget to add his tail.

Pluto's ears can act together to accentuate a mood or an expressive pose.

STEP 5

Erase your guidelines and clean up the drawing.

His collar hangs loosely at the back of his neck.

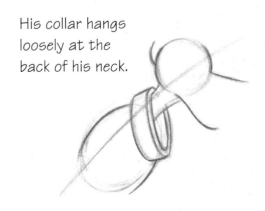

STEP 6

Now color your drawing of Pluto.

29

COLORING STYLES

You can color your drawings in many different ways.

Some artists like pastels.

Be careful! You don't want to make a mess the way Goofy does.

Your final picture will look different depending on how you choose to color it.

You can always use crayons or colored pencils. Then maybe add some paint.

Watercolors and tempera paints can be fun too!

31

GOOD LUCK boys and girls!

Now that you've learned how to draw your favorite characters, try experimenting on your own. Remember to use your imagination—and have fun!

Drawing